COIN & BANKNOTE TRICKS

BRUCE SMITH

ARCTURUS

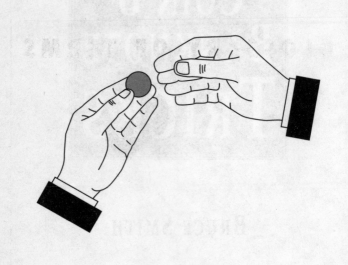

GLOSSARY OF TERMS

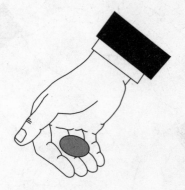

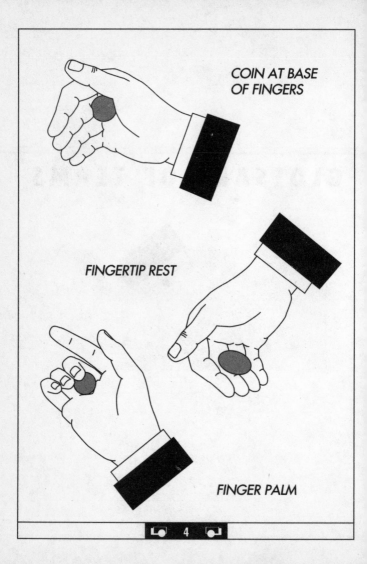

COIN AT BASE
OF FINGERS

FINGERTIP REST

FINGER PALM

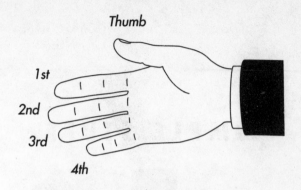

Thumb

1st
2nd
3rd
4th

FACE OF
BANKNOTE

10

BACK OF
BANKNOTE

10

SIMPLE STUFF

Effect *A coin vanishes from the magician's right hand to appear in the left.*

Requirements *Any two coins.*

Preparation *None.*

• • • • • • • • • • • • • • • •

1 Show a coin on the palm of each hand (illustration 1). The coin in the left hand should be below the third and fourth fingers. The one in the right hand should be at the base of the thumb. Hold the hands 30cm/12in apart on a table top.

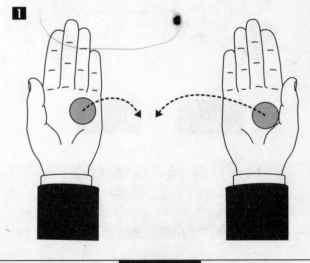

2 At exactly the same time turn both hands over quickly so that the thumbs come close together. As you do this the coin from the right hand will be thrown under the left hand (illustration 2), but to the audience it appears that you have just turned your hands over and there is a coin under each one.

3 Lift your right hand to show that the coin has vanished. Lift the left hand to show that amazingly there are now two coins under it.

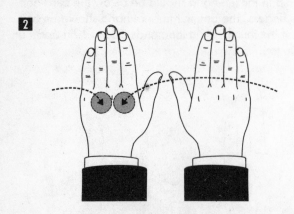

TOP TIPS FOR TRICKSTERS

Money magic is always more effective if the coins or banknotes used in the trick are borrowed from trustworthy members of the audience.

Effect *This is not a magic trick, but a stunt or "scam" you can try on your friends, using a banknote, to prove that there is no such thing as "easy money". If you use their money perhaps you can make a profit!*

Requirements *Any banknote.*

Preparation *None.*

• • • • • • • • • • • • • • • •

1 The right thumb and first finger hold a note vertically at the middle of the right long edge. The open left hand is in position at the middle of the left long edge, but the left hand must not touch the note (illustration 1).

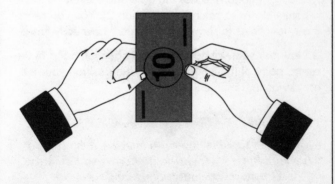

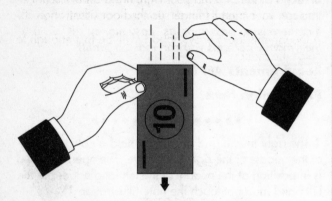

2 The right hand releases the note and the left hand instantly closes to catch it (illustration 2). You can repeat this a few times to show your "punter" how easy this is.

3 Now ask your friend to hold his open left hand at the centre point of the left long side – the position your left hand was in a moment ago.

TOP TIPS FOR TRICKSTERS

Tricks with coins are fine for showing a few people close up, but – with a few exceptions (like the "Miser's Dream") – are not really suitable on stage.

4 Tell them that if they catch the bill they can keep it!

5 Let go of the bill with your right hand and watch it slip through your friend's fingers to the floor (illustration 3).

Although this looks easy, nobody will be fast enough to catch the money.

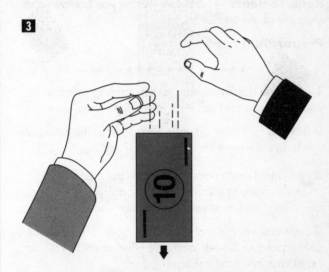

TOP TIPS FOR TRICKSTERS

If you do perform coin productions on a stage it is worth while having the coins silver plated so that they will shine in the stage lights and be easier to see.

Effect *A banknote is borrowed and rolled up into a tight tube. When it is handed to a member of the audience the note vanishes. It reappears in the magician's pocket.*

Requirements *A banknote (which you borrow from a member of the audience).*

Preparation *None.*

● ● ● ● ● ● ● ● ● ● ● ● ● ● ● ●

1 Borrow a banknote from a rich, trusting member of your audience and roll it up into a tight tube.

2 Stand a spectator on your left and hold the banknote tightly in your right hand to stop it unrolling.

1

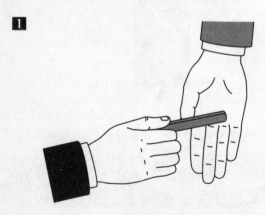

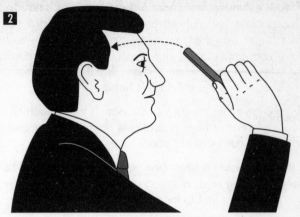

3 Ask the spectator to hold out their right hand palm up.
With your left hand hold on to their right wrist.

4 Lift the note up and bring it down to tap the
spectator's open hand (illustration 1). Explain that on the
count of three the spectator must close their hand
around the note.

5 Swing your right hand up in an arc to the right of
your face (illustration 2) and back down. Count "one"
as the note taps their open hand. Repeat this action and
count "two" as you tap their palm again.

6 The next time your hand swings up, you leave the
rolled up note tucked behind your ear. The timing must
be the same as before – the right hand swings back
down as though nothing has happened.

7 Your extended first finger hits the spectator's hand. The spectator will instinctively close their hand around your finger. Ask them to open their hand so that you can have your finger back! This creates an amusing situation for a few moments when it seems that the money has vanished inside the spectator's hand.

8 You can either reveal that the note is tucked behind your right ear or have a duplicate note in your pocket which you can return to your money lender.

The effect makes a great bar bet and stunt, and can be used as a gag or as a strong piece of magic. However, it is not really suitable for a stage presentation.

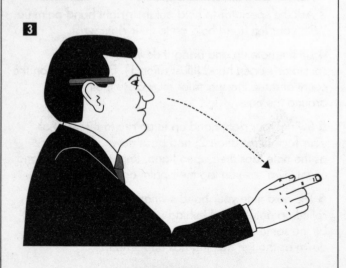

BASIC
SLEIGHT-OF-HAND
VANISHES

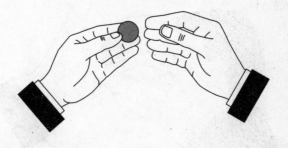

Effect *A coin vanishes.*

Requirements *Any coin.*

Preparation *None.*

• • • • • • • • • • • • • • • •

1 Display the coin lying at the base of your right fingers.

2 Rest the edge of your right little finger across your left fingers (illustration 1).

1

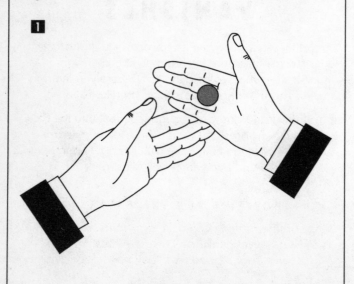

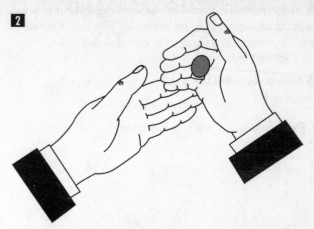

3 Pivot the right hand inward towards you, apparently to tip the coin into your left hand. In fact your right fingers curl inwards to hold the coin securely in the right fingers. This is the finger palm position (illustration 2).

4 Your left hand closes as though it did contain the coin. It moves downwards and turns over, drawing the audience's attention to it. Point with the right hand and move the left hand away to the left (illustration 3).

TOP TIPS FOR TRICKSTERS

If you are performing any coin tricks remember that the audience's attention will be on your hands. Ensure that you give them a good wash before you perform!

5 You can now casually lower your right hand to your side as attention is on the left hand. Slip the coin into your right pocket or keep it finger-palmed to be reproduced later.

6 Slowly open the left hand to show the coin has vanished.

3

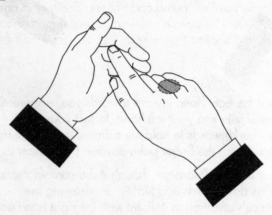

Effect *A coin vanishes.*

Requirements *Any coin.*

Preparation *None.*

● ● ● ● ● ● ● ● ● ● ● ● ● ● ● ●

1 Hold the coin horizontally, parallel with the floor, with the tips of your left thumb and fingers. The fingers and thumb should be pointing upwards. Your fingers should be held together so that nobody can see between them.

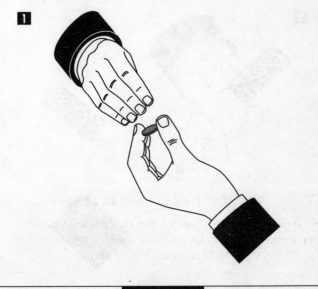

2 Your right hand approaches from behind to apparently pick up the coin (illustration 1). Your right thumb goes under the coin and your right fingers come over the top.

3 As soon as your right fingers cover the coin from view your left thumb releases the coin, allowing it to fall to the base of your left fingers (illustration 2).

4 However, your right hand continues as though it did contain the coin. It clenches into a fist and moves upwards and away to the right (illustration 3). It is important that you watch the right hand move and hold

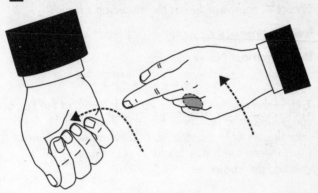

the left hand still. The rules of misdirection to remember here are first, that the audience will watch a moving object, and second, they will look where you look.

5 Close the left hand, clipping the coin at the base of the left fingers (finger palm position).

6 Open your right hand to show that the coin has vanished!

TOP TIPS FOR TRICKSTERS

It is worth while washing your hands before and after you practise as coins can become grubby and dirty very easily.

Effect *A coin vanishes in the magician's hands.*

Requirements *Any coin.*

Preparation *None.*

• • • • • • • • • • • • • • • •

1 Hold the coin vertically in your left hand, at the tips of your thumb and first three fingers (illustration 1). Keep your fingers tight together so that the audience cannot see between them. The backs of your fingers are towards the audience.

1

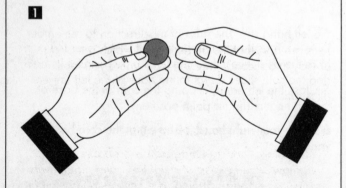

2 The right hand reaches over as though to take the coin from the left hand. The right thumb goes behind the coin and the right fingers cover it at the front.

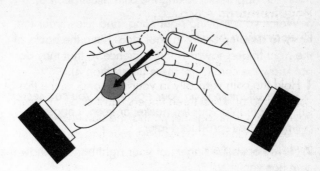

2

3 As soon as the right fingers completely cover the coin from the audience's view the left thumb releases its hold, and the coin slides down to the base of the left fingers (illustration 2).

DAVID ROTH

This New York coin magician is probably today's acknowledged expert at sleight-of-hand magic with coins. Many of his routines are described in detail in the book, David Roth's Expert Coin Magic, written, illustrated and published by Richard Kaufman and available from most good magic shops.

4 The left hand curls slightly to hold the coin in the finger palm position while the right hand moves away to the right, apparently taking the coin (illustration 3).

5 Watch your moving right hand, and allow your left hand to drop naturally to your side. Keep the backs of the right fingers towards the audience so that they do not know the coin is not there (illustration 4).

6 While attention is on your right hand you can secretly slip the coin into your left pocket or keep it finger palmed to be reproduced later.

7 Slowly open the fingers of your right hand to show the coin has vanished!

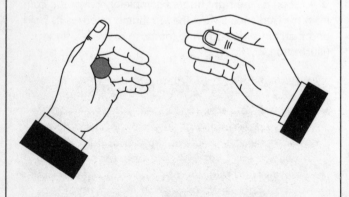

4

CHUNG LING SOO (1861-1918)

One of the highlights of Chung Ling Soo's spectacular show was the "Dream of Wealth". From mid-air he produced coins, banknotes and a cheque for one million pounds! Although known as the Marvellous Chinese Conjurer, the oriental character was actually a disguise for William E. Robinson who was really born in America! He was fatally wounded on stage during a performance of the famous "Catching a Bullet".

PRODUCTIONS

Effect *The magician shows a banknote, folds it into a tube and tips out a genuine coin!*

Requirements *Any banknote and coin.*

Preparation *Place the coin and banknote in your pocket so that they can easily be removed together.*

● ● ● ● ● ● ● ● ● ● ● ● ● ● ● ●

1 Reach into your pocket and remove the banknote and coin, ensuring that the coin is kept concealed behind the note. Explain to the audience that this is your private Money Making Machine!

2 Hold up the note with the right hand, holding the hidden coin clipped to the back of the note with the right thumb (illustration 1).

3 Snap the left side of the note with the left fingers. This proves to the audience that the left hand is empty and that nothing is concealed behind the left side of the banknote.

TOP TIPS FOR TRICKSTERS

Gimmicked and fake coins will enable you to do many more tricks – but it is essential to master the basics of sleight-of-hand magic first.

3

4 Hold the left side of the note in the left hand mirroring the right hand's grip. Bring the two hands together making the note bend as in illustration 2. Secretly transfer the coin from under the right thumb to under the left thumb. Flick the right side of the bill with the right first finger (illustration 3).

PAUL DANIELS (b. 1938)

Paul Daniels is Britain's best known magician, due to his many series of The Paul Daniels Magic Show on BBC1 and his live performances in theatres around the country. One of his most memorable television performances was the day he made £1,000,000 cash vanish – and reappear! Watching over him on that occasion was newspaper tycoon Robert Maxwell!

5 Fold the note into a tube, secretly wrapping the concealed coin inside.

6 Tilt the opening in the folded note downwards so that the coin slowly falls out (illustration 4). You have proved that you have made your own Money Making Machine!

FRED KAPS (1926-1980)

This Dutch magician was a master of sleight of hand and manipulation. He was a winner of many famous magical awards – a true World Champion. His act featured the manipulation of banknotes and giant coins, and concluded with the production of an almost endless stream of salt pouring from his fist.

Effect *The magician displays at his fingertips a coin of small denomination (for example, a penny). With a magical pass the magician changes it into two coins, both of a much higher value than the original coin!*

Requirements *Three coins (one small and two large).*

Preparation *The two large coins are held upright near the tips of your right thumb and first finger. They are secretly hidden by the smaller coin which you hold upright and at right angles to them, also at the tips of the right thumb and first finger (illustration 1). Hold this set-up in front of a mirror and you will see that the two*

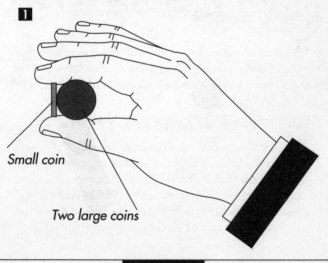

Small coin

Two large coins

large coins are hidden. Practise the following routine many times in front of a mirror watching it from different angles until you are confident the large coins are completely hidden.

Set up the coins in position and you are ready to begin your performance.

● ● ● ● ● ● ● ● ● ● ● ● ● ● ●

1 Hold up the right hand to show the small coin face on and at the audience's eye level so that they cannot see the two extra coins (illustration 2). The trick will only work if the coin is held at the height of the audience's line of vision. It is important that the edges of the large coins are at the exact centre of the small coin, to give as much cover as possible.

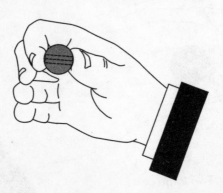

3

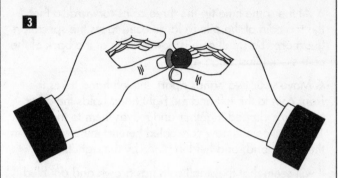

2 The audience have, apparently, seen that your right hand is empty, except for the small coin. Now show both sides of your left hand to prove it is empty.

3 Bring the two hands together with the first fingers and thumbs of both hands pointing towards each other. Again it is essential that the hands stay level with the audience's eye level so they do not see the extra coins.

4 Your left thumb goes beneath the coins, pushing on the bottom edge of the small coin (illustration 3), pivoting it on to the bottom of the two large coins so that all three coins are now in one stack.

TOP TIPS FOR TRICKSTERS

It is a good idea to keep a set of coins especially for performing with. Keep these polished and clean to improve your "professional" image.

5 At the same time tip the three coins forward so that the top coin of the pile (a large coin) faces the spectators head on. The small coin is now hidden at the back of the coin stack (illustration 4).

6 Move your two hands apart; the left hand takes the front coin to the left and the right hand holds the other two coins clipped together and moves them to the right. The small coin is now concealed behind the large coin in the right hand, and held in place by the right thumb.

It will seem that the small coin has grown and doubled in an instant. As you put the coins away be careful not to expose the small hidden coin.

This is a quick visual effect which is ideal for a one-to-one performance, especially when creating extra change at the shop, bank or on the bus!

4

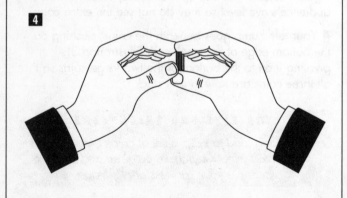

CONTINUOUS COINS

Effect *The magician borrows a handkerchief from a spectator and produces an apparently endless stream of coins from within its folds.*

Requirements *A large cotton handkerchief (preferably borrowed from a member of the audience) and two identical coins – the larger the better.*

Preparation *Place one coin in your left trouser pocket and one in your right trouser pocket. You are all set to produce money from nothing!*

. . . .

1

1 Borrow the handkerchief and show it on both sides. Show both your hands are empty so there is no suspicion of you sneaking anything into the handkerchief.

2 Point the fingers and thumb of your right hand upwards with all the tips touching. Your left hand drapes the handkerchief over your right hand so that the pointed fingers are in the centre of the handkerchief.

3 Show your left hand is empty and, with the left hand, grasp the centre of the handkerchief and lift it up. You are going to exchange the positions of your hands so that your left hand is under the handkerchief and your right hand is uncovered. Flip the handkerchief with your right hand and throw it over the left hand. The left hand takes position with the fingers pointing up (illustration 1).

2

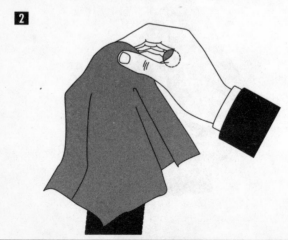

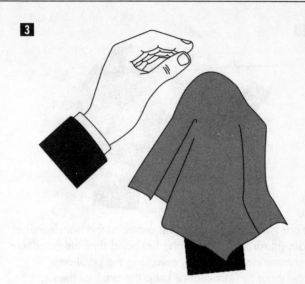

4 You say that you can see something sticking out of the top of the handkerchief, apparently held by the left fingertips. With your right hand you mime taking the object, keeping the back of the hand towards the audience so they cannot see if you have taken anything or not.

5 Place the right hand in your righthand pocket, apparently to dispose of the object. In fact you finger palm the coin in your pocket. The audience's impression should be that you are putting something in your pocket, *not* secretly removing something!

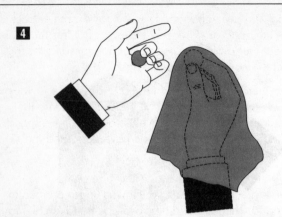

6 Your right hand grasps the centre of the handkerchief again (illustration 2) and the left hand flips the handkerchief over the right hand, reversing the positions. Throughout this procedure keep the back of the right hand towards the audience so that the concealed coin remains hidden.

7 Again pretend there is an object in the centre of the handkerchief and mime taking it with the left hand (illustration 3). Your left hand goes to the left pocket to apparently dispose of the object. In fact it finger palms the coin there and reappears with the coin concealed.

8 The left fingers take hold of the centre of the handkerchief – and, through the material, of the coin in the right hand. The coin in the left hand remains hidden in the finger palm position (illustration 4).

9 The now empty right hand flips the handkerchief back over the left hand as described in step 3. But this time you reveal that a coin has magically appeared in the centre of the handkerchief (illustration 5)!

10 Take the coin in your right hand and place it in your right pocket. In your pocket slide the coin back into the finger palm position and remove the apparently empty right hand. It will appear that you have deposited the coin in your pocket.

11 Now the right hand grasps the centre of the handkerchief – and the coin which was finger palmed in the left hand. The left hand flips over the handkerchief to show another coin has appeared (illustration 6)!

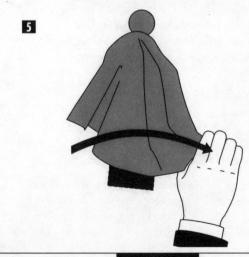

5

12 The left hand takes the coin and places it in the left pocket where you slide it back into finger palm!

13 By repeating steps 8 through to 12 you can produce an apparently endless stream of coins from within the folds of the handkerchief – just by reproducing the same two coins.

When you think you have profited enough, return the handkerchief to its owner and take your applause.

There is plenty of potential for humour with this effect as you pretend that the owner has got a coin trapped in the folds of their handkerchief. . . and another. . . and another. . . which you keep pocketing until you return the handkerchief!

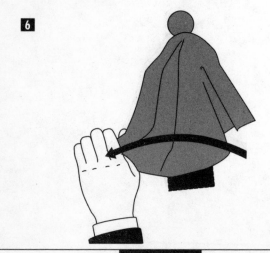

6

Effect This is one of the true classics of coin magic, performed by professional magicians all over the world. The magician plucks coins from the air and drops them into a container. In the finale the magician's hands are full of a stream of gleaming coins caught in mid-air.

Requirements A special fake coin, a stack of genuine identical coins (about 25), a container (a large tin or a small plastic bucket) and a special holder.

Preparation The special coin is made by drilling a hole in a small metal disc the same size as the coins (a blank pet's name tag is ideal for this as it already has

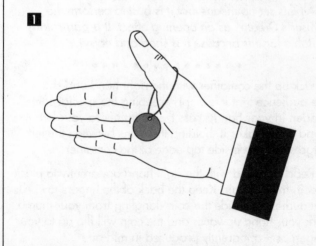

the hole in it). Thread a small loop of cotton through the hole so that it will loop over your thumb (illustration 1).

The special holder is made from an old sock! This will hold the stack of coins that will make your big final production (about 12). To make the holder cut off the toe of the sock and sew around the edge of the hole with elastic (illustration 2). Put half the coins inside the sock – the elastic should prevent them falling out – and safety pin it under your jacket or coat on your right side.

Your final preparation is to loop the thread on the fake coin over your right thumb and stack the remaining coins (about 12) in your closed left hand. The empty container should be on your table.

All this set-up means that it is best to perform the "Miser's Dream" as an opening effect. It is particularly suitable for this because it is short and noisy!.

● ● ● ● ● ● ● ● ● ● ● ● ● ● ●

1 Pick up the container with the right hand and show the audience that it is empty (keeping the special coin hidden in your hand). Pass the container to your left hand which takes it, holding the coins between the left fingers and the inside top edge of the container.

2 Reach forward with the right hand apparently to pluck a coin from the air. Keep the back of the fingers towards the audience to hide the coin dangling from your thumb. Jerk your hand upwards and the coin will flip up to your fingertips – apparently produced in mid-air.

2

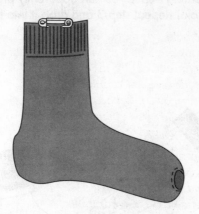

3 Move the right hand to the top of the container and apparently drop the coin inside. What really happens is that you release the coin and it returns to its position dangling around the thumb. At the same time your left fingers allow one coin inside the container to drop to the bottom – the audience will hear it drop. If the timing is right this is very convincing – it seems as though you have just dropped a coin into the container.

TOP TIPS FOR TRICKSTERS

Many fake and gimmicked coins are available from magic shops, dealers and suppliers. You may find a magic shop listed in your local Yellow Pages.

4 By repeating step 2 you can apparently produce another coin! Repeat step 3 and drop it into the container.

TOP TIPS FOR TRICKSTERS

You can have great fun with money magic at any time. When out shopping you can produce the correct change from mid-air or vanish a note as you hand it to the bank cashier!

5 Continue producing coins until all the coins in your left hand have been dropped into the container. You can produce coins from behind your knee, under your armpit or from your audience! It is a very funny situation to apparently produce coins from behind a spectator's ears, or beard and so on.

6 When the last coin has been dropped, allow your right hand to fall naturally to your side as you shake the container noisily and perhaps jokingly ask if anyone would like to contribute to your collection! While the audience's attention is on the container, your right hand reaches under the right side of your jacket and squeezes the coins out of the holder. Any noise made while you're doing this will be covered by you rattling the container in your left hand.

7 Finally place the container on the table or the floor and open your right hand, letting the final big production of coins stream from your hand into the container (illustration 3). The special coin will fall unnoticed among the regular coins.

STREET MAGICIANS

Many magicians began their performing lives "on the street" as buskers, trying to extract money from the passers-by. Ex-street magicians enjoying great success today include Harry Anderson, John Lenahan, Keith Fields, Leo Ward and Penn and Teller.

Effect *This is an alternative way of producing the single coin in your right hand when you are performing the "Miser's Dream". It uses a regular coin.*

Requirements *Any coin.*

Preparation *None.*

● ● ● ● ● ● ● ● ● ● ● ● ● ● ● ● ●

1 The coin begins in the "thumb clip" position (illustration 1). The coin is clipped between the base of the right thumb and the first finger. The coin is hidden from the audience as throughout the routine the back of the right hand faces the audience.

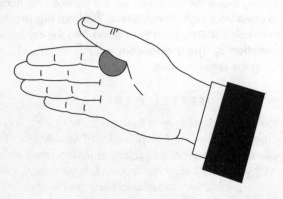

2 The four right fingers all bend inwards (illustration 2). The first finger goes behind the coin and the second finger in front as they clip the coin.

3 To produce the coin the fingers open out again, the first and second fingers bringing the coin into view clipped between them (illustration 3).

TOP TIPS FOR TRICKSTERS

The most important thing in coin magic is to make your hand look natural when it is secretly concealing a coin. If your hand looks tense and cramped it will be noticed. The best advice is to keep a coin "palmed" in your hand all day so that you forget about it – it will help you to act more naturally during a performance.

3

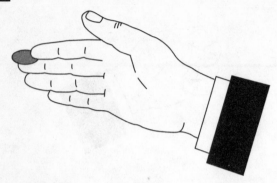

4 To apparently drop the coin into the container simply reverse the procedure. As the right hand moves over to the container, the right fingers close and the right thumb clips the coin again. The right fingers can now be spread and shown to be empty. The coin can then be produced again. . . and again. . . and again.

AL GOSHMAN (1921-1991)

New York magician Al Goshman was one of the first and finest close-up magicians. Until his death he was one of the resident magicians at the Magic Castle in Hollywood. Throughout his act, if you said "please", he would produce a successsion of coins from beneath a salt cellar – each coin bigger than the last.

PENETRATIONS

Effect *The magician places a coin in the left fist. When he slaps the back of the fist with his right hand the coin appears on top of his fist, having apparently penetrated his hand!*

Requirements *Any coin.*

Preparation *None.*

● ● ● ● ● ● ● ● ● ● ● ● ● ● ● ● ●

1

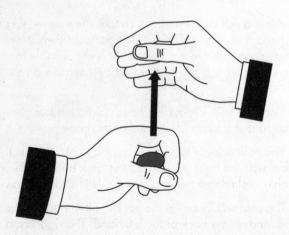

This is a quick visual stunt which looks like clever sleight of hand, but relies more on a special knack which will only take a few minutes to learn. It is not suitable for a big show, but it is fun to do for a few friends with a borrowed coin.

1 Place the coin in your left hand. Close the hand around it in a loose fist, turned palm down.

2 You now appear to simply slap the back of the left hand with the right. As you do this, jerk both hands up slightly and release the coin from the left fist (illustration 1).

3 The coin will fly out of the left fist, hit the right palm and land on the back of the left hand. The right hand then slaps the back of the left, holding the coin in place (illustration 2).

4 Lift the right hand off the left fist to show that the coin has apparently penetrated the hand and landed on the back of the left hand (illustration 3).

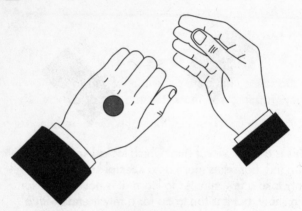

Effect *The magician passes a borrowed coin through his right leg!*

Requirements *Any coin (preferably borrowed) and a right leg that is wearing trousers!*

Preparation *None.*

• • • • • • • • • • • • • • • •

1 Borrow a coin from a member of your audience. If they wish they can mark it with a pen or crayon.

2 Hold the coin between the right thumb and fingers.

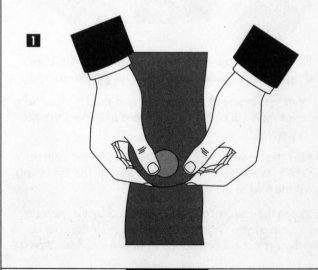

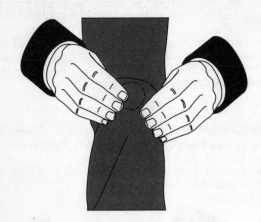

3 Place the coin on your right leg just above the knee. The right thumb holds the coin against your trouser leg.

4 With the fingers of both the left and right hands fold a piece of material of the trousers up and under the coin (illustration 1).

5 Fold the material you have pulled under the coin up and over to cover the coin (illustration 2). The left thumb holds the fold of material in position.

6 When the coin is completely covered by the material the thumb of your right hand secretly pulls the coin up into the right hand behind the right fingers (illustration 3).

7 Your right hand now curls slightly to finger palm the coin. Move your right hand around to the back of the right leg. The left fingers keep hold of the fold of trouser material which is apparently trapping the coin.

8 Release your left hand's grip on the material. It will drop, revealing that the coin has gone. Turn your left hand around to show that it is empty.

9 With your right hand, remove the coin from behind the right knee by pushing the coin from the finger palm position up to the fingertips. It appears that the coin passed through your leg!

This is a great trick for an impromptu performance for just a few people.

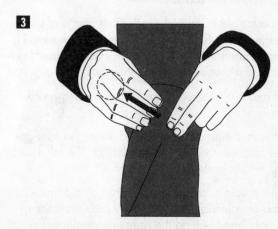

Effect The magician gives a spectator seven coins to hold. Despite the fact that the spectator holds the coins tightly inside their fist, the magician makes one coin penetrate through the spectator's hand.

Requirements Seven coins of identical value.

Preparation None.

● ● ● ● ● ● ● ● ● ● ● ● ● ● ● ●

1 Hold the coins in your cupped left hand and stand facing the spectator who is going to assist you.

2 Ask the spectator to hold out their hand palm up ready to receive the coins.

3 With your right hand pick up the first coin and place it in the spectator's hand counting "one" (illustration 1). Continue to count the next four coins, allowing each one to click against a coin already in their hand – this gets

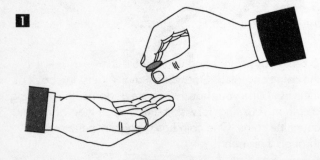

1

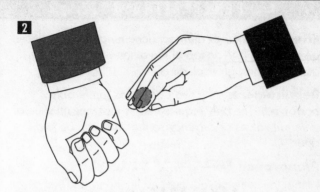

them used to hearing the coin go into their hand. This will allow you to "short change" them in the next step.

4 When you place the sixth coin in the spectator's hand simply click it against a coin already in their hand, but do not let go of it. Keep it gripped between the right thumb and first finger. Make sure that the coin remains concealed by your right fingers.

5 Throw the final coin from your left hand straight into the spectator's right hand. They will snap their fist closed (illustration 2).

6 Bring your right hand underneath their fist, keeping the coin concealed. Slap your hand against the back of their fist. Slide your hand out from underneath revealing a coin in your fingers. Ask them to open their hand and count the coins. One coin has magically penetrated through their hand!

Effect *Two notes of different denominations are placed on the table, one on top of the other. Magically they penetrate through each other.*

Requirements *Any two banknotes (preferably borrowed). The only requirement is that they must be of different values or currency so that they can be told apart.*

Preparation *None.*

●●●●●●●●●●●●●●●●●

1 Lay the two notes on the table to form a V. The point of the V is towards you. The lower note is angled away

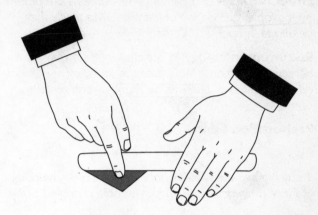

to your left and the upper note angled away to your right. It is important that the note on top is slightly further forward toward the audience. It does not quite meet the edges of the lower note.

2 Make sure the audience is clear which note is on top.

3 Beginning at the point of the V use your two first fingers to start rolling the notes together (illustration 1).

4 Continue rolling until only a small part of a corner of the lower note is visible on the table. When you reach this point stop rolling. More of the upper note will be sticking out as it began slightly further forward.

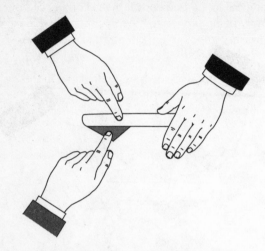

3

5 Cover the visible corner of the lower note with your left hand. Do this while your right finger points to the corner of the upper note sticking out on the right (illustration 2). Ask a spectator to place a finger on the corner on your right (illustration 3).

6 As they do this, secretly roll the notes forward slightly. Under cover of your left hand, the left corner will flip around the roll – it will go under the rolled up notes and flip back on to the table in its original position. This is the secret move which makes the trick work.

7 Lift your left hand and ask the spectator to place a finger from their other hand on that corner.

8 Point out to the audience that the corners of both notes are now being pinned to the table. Explain this makes any trickery impossible – unknown to them it has already happened!

9 Unroll the notes towards you and show that – incredibly – the two notes have passed through each other. The note that was on top is now below (illustration 4).

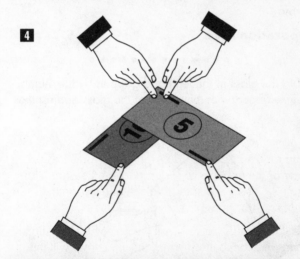

TOP TIPS FOR TRICKSTERS

With a few well practised coin tricks which you can perform with any coins you will always be able to entertain friends any time, any place, anywhere!

Effect A borrowed coin penetrates through the bottom of a glass tumbler, ending up trapped inside.

Requirements Any coin (the heavier the better) and a smooth-sided glass tumbler. It is more effective if these are both borrowed. This is a great trick to do in a bar or at the dinner table with an empty glass that is sitting nearby.

Preparation None.

• • • • • • • • • • • • • • • •

1 Hold the glass in the left hand gripped by the thumb and little finger, with the mouth of the glass against the

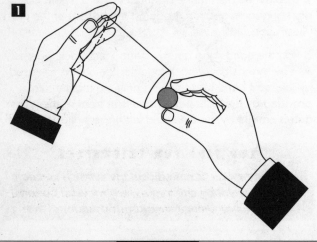

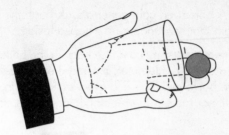

left palm. It is important that the other fingers can be moved without disturbing the grip on the glass.

2 Display the coin in the right hand. Hold it with the right fingertips and tap it against the bottom of the glass (illustration 1).

3 Part the hands and quickly bring them back together. As your hands come back together the coin is released by the right hand and, moving with the momentum provided by the right hand, travels in front of the glass and is caught by the extended left fingers (illustration 2).

TOP TIPS FOR TRICKSTERS

Money magic is not particularly suitable for an audience of young children as they may not be familiar with currency or its value.

3

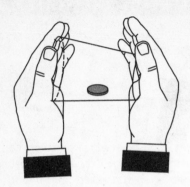

4 As soon as the left hand catches the coin it moves to the left, then jerks back to the right causing the coin to fly inside the glass. At the same time the right hand slaps against the bottom of the glass (illustration 3).

5 Because the coin travels too fast for the eye to follow, it appears to the audience that the coin has visibly penetrated through the bottom of the glass.

PENN AND TELLER

This outrageous American duo have shocked audiences around the world with their "sick tricks" and upset many magicians. They began their performing careers as street entertainers and are now in demand for TV shows and live performances – and have even made their own movie – Penn and Teller Get Killed.

Effect *An empty matchbox is shown and placed in the centre of the table. The magician places a coin under the table. The coin vanishes from under the table and can be heard appearing inside the closed matchbox!*

Requirements *A regular matchbox and two identical coins.*

Preparation *Slide one of the coins between the bottom of the tray and the outer cover. Close the matchbox, keeping the coin concealed in its hiding place (illustration 1).*

● ● ● ● ● ● ● ● ● ● ● ● ● ● ● ● ●

1

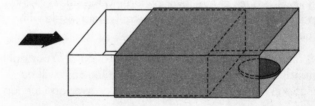

1 Slide out the drawer of the matchbox with the left hand. Hold the outside of the cover with the right hand, palm up.

2 As the drawer slides out, move your right thumb inside the cover on top of the concealed coin (illustration 2).

3 Pull the drawer out of the cover and show it is empty. Show the back of the cover by turning the right hand palm down, keeping the coin secretly held inside with the right thumb.

4 Slide the drawer back inside (illustration 3). Your right hand is still palm down and therefore the coin will be trapped between the top edge of the drawer and the top

TOP TIPS FOR TRICKSTERS

Be warned! When people discover you are a magician they may say, "If you're a magician produce some money then!" Now you can!

of the cover (illustration 4). While the drawer is open the coin will stay in this position, but when pushed shut the coin will be heard dropping into the drawer. Place the box with the open drawer on the centre of the table.

5 Take the duplicate coin under the table with your right hand and tap it against the underside of the table. Show that your left hand is empty and lift up the matchbox from the table.

6 Under the table your right hand slides the coin into your sock!

7 The left hand brings the matchbox down on the table and at the same time pushes the drawer closed. The coin can be heard dropping inside the matchbox.

3

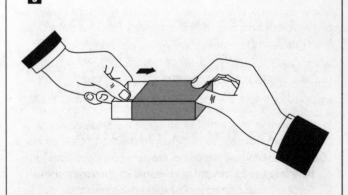

8 Bring out your right hand to show it is empty, and ask someone to open the box to prove that the coin really has arrived inside.

4

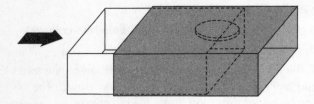

T. NELSON DOWNS (1867-1938)

T. Nelson Downs was an American magician who billed himself as the "King of Koins" (sic). As a railway clerk he spent his spare time learning sleight of hand with coins and creating his own variations. He turned professional and almost overnight became a big vaudeville star with his unique and original act of apparently producing coins from mid-air. One of his most challenging moves is the "Downs Coin Star" in which coins balanced on the tips of the four fingers and thumb vanish and re-appear.

Effect The magician covers a coin on the table with a glass. To conceal the coin the glass is covered with a napkin. The magician says that the coin is going to vanish. This doesn't happen, but when a spectator slaps down on the napkin-covered glass it squashes flat! The glass has penetrated through the table!

Requirements A smooth-sided drinking glass, two paper napkins and any coin (this could be borrowed).

Preparation For this effect to work you must be sitting at a table. Prepare by setting the props out in front of you on the table.

• • • • • • • • • • • • • • • •

1

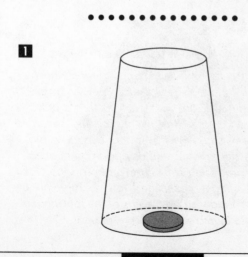

1 Explain to the audience that you are going to attempt to pass a solid object through the table top.

2 Place the coin on the table about 30cm/12in from the rear edge and cover it with the upturned glass, isolating the coin inside (illustration 1).

3 Open out the two napkins and lay them on top of each other covering the glass (illustration 2). Explain to the audience, "The coin must be covered to keep the secret!"

4 Pull the napkins down around the outside of the glass to show its outline and with one hand twist the glass tightly inside the napkins to show its shape more clearly (illustration 3).

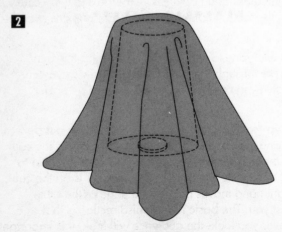

2

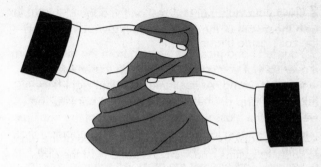

5 Lift the glass and napkins together to show the coin is still on the table. Replace the glass and napkins over the coin.

6 Ask everyone to concentrate on making the coin penetrate through the solid table. If you wish you can even get everyone to hold hands to form a "power circle"!

7 Lift up the glass and napkins together with the right hand and look suprised and disappointed that the coin is still there. Your left hand moves towards the coin to pick it up. While the audience's attention is on the coin, the right hand moves back to the edge of the table nearest you. The basic rule of misdirection is that wherever you look, the audience will look. It is important throughout the next few steps that you keep looking at the coin, not at your right hand.

8 Bring your right hand to rest on the edge of the table with the mouth of the glass pointing towards your lap.

9 Your left hand picks up the coin from the table to turn it over so that you can look at it more carefully to see what went wrong. At the same time your right fingers relax their grip on the glass through the napkin. The weight of the glass will make it slide out of the napkins into your waiting lap (illustration 4)! It is important that you lift your heels off the floor slightly to make your lap a "valley". This ensures the glass will roll into your lap and not on to the floor!

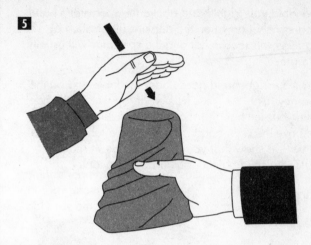

10 Hold the napkins gently in the right hand so that they keep the shape of the glass even though it is no longer there!

11 The left hand places the coin back in the centre of the table and the right hand covers it with the napkins as though they still contained the glass. To the audience it should appear that nothing has changed – the big suprise is coming in a moment!

12 "It didn't work," you say, "because I forgot to get someone to tap the top of the glass." Ask a member of the audience to hold their hand just above the napkins (illustration 5). Try to get someone for this who you think will respond loudly to the surprise.

13 Hold your right hand above the spectator's hand and smash it down on the napkins (illustration 6). The napkins will squash flat and the spectator will usually scream!

14 Your right hand goes under the table and on the journey takes the glass from your lap. Lift up the napkins with your left hand to show that the coin is still there. Remove the right hand from under the table with the glass – to show that you did as you promised and passed a solid object right through the table!

6

TOP TIPS FOR TRICKSTERS

Even the most famous stage illusionists know a few small coin tricks that they can perform to maintain their reputation when off-stage!

FEATURE ITEMS

Effect *This is in the miracle class, and when well rehearsed will make a great finale to any act or show you are putting on.*

A borrowed coin is marked. It vanishes while held by a member of the audience and appears inside a sealed matchbox which is wrapped in the centre of a ball of wool!

Requirements *A ball of heavy knitting wool, a regular sized matchbox, a large clear container (big enough to hold the ball of wool), four elastic bands, a special handkerchief and a special coin slide.*

Preparation *The handkerchief is made from any cotton handkerchief with a coin secretly sewn into one corner.*

1

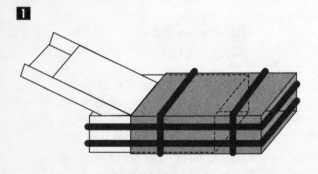

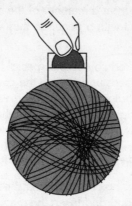

2

The coin slide is made from any piece of flat metal or cardboard. This is folded into a flat tube so that a coin can be dropped into one end and will slide down and out the other end. This is the secret prop for this effect.

Insert one end of the slide into the open drawer of the empty matchbox and wrap the four elastic bands around the matchbox as in illustration 1. The bands will hold the slide in position and close the box when the slide is removed.

Wrap the wool around the matchbox to form a ball with the matchbox hidden inside. Make sure the wool is not wrapped too tightly otherwise the slide may get stuck when you have to remove it at the crucial moment.

Place the prepared ball of wool out of sight on your table – inside a hat or large box is best.

1 Borrow a coin from a member of the audience and have them mark it with a pencil so they will recognise it in the future.

2 Wrap the marked coin in the special handkerchief. What really happens underneath the cover of the handkerchief is that you keep the borrowed coin finger-palmed in your right hand, and hand the secret sewn-in coin to a member of the audience to hold through the folds of the material. They will believe they are holding the borrowed coin wrapped inside the handkerchief.

3 Reach into your box (or wherever the ball of wool is) with your right hand and insert the marked coin in the coin slide (illustration 2). The coin will slide down into

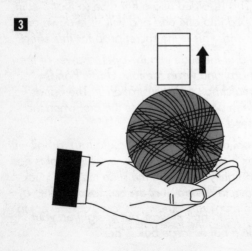

3

4

the matchbox wrapped inside the ball of wool. Pull the slide out of the ball of wool, leaving it in the box. Remove the ball of wool and put it in the clear container. Hand this to a spectator to hold.

4 Ask your "hanky holding helper" to stand up, and ask them if they are still holding on to the coin. After they have answered "yes" whip the handkerchief out of their hand and display it on both sides to show that the coin has vanished.

TOP TIPS FOR TRICKSTERS

The most important tip – which has been broken by every coin magician I know – is to be careful not to spend the fake coins you buy!

5 Ask the spectator holding the ball of wool to stand up and face the audience. Hand the end of the wool to the spectator who lent you the coin, and ask them to pull it (illustration 4). As they pull on the end, the ball of wool will twist and turn inside the container.

6 When the wool has all been unwound, the audience will see the matchbox inside the container. Ask another spectator to remove the box (illustration 5). Emphasise that at no point have you touched the box. Ask them to remove the rubber bands and open the box.

7 Inside the drawer is the actual marked coin that vanished moments before! Have the coin returned to its owner for verification and take your applause.

5